MW00581924

Celebration of Life

A LEGACY JOURNAL

Celebration of Life

A Legacy Journal

By

Sharon Purtill

Published by Dunhill-Clare Publishing - Ontario, Canada

Copyright © 2019 Dunhill-Clare Publishing - All rights reserved.

dunhillclare@gmail.com

First Published in 2019

Paperback ISBN: 978-0-9734104-3-3

First Edition

Library and Archives Canada Cataloguing in Publication

Printed in the United States of America

Author's Note

Welcome to your *Celebration of Life: A Legacy Journal*. This one-of-a-kind journal came to be rather unexpectedly while I was on holidays with my parents. The three of us were sitting around chatting one afternoon when I began reflecting on how much I knew or rather didn't know about their lives from their perspective.

Although my parents and I have had decades of time together (they are both in their eighties), I realized I had no idea what they consider their greatest accomplishments to be. Who has been the most influential person in their life? What has brought them the most joy? What has been their proudest moment? How about a time they experienced their greatest fear? And what do they know about our family history that I don't know? Perhaps more importantly, I wondered what unfulfilled goals and dreams they had. What life lessons could they share with me, and what do they want their legacy to look like?

My curiosity led me to pull out my laptop and open up a blank document. I began to record some of the questions I had been pondering and it was in that moment that this journal was born. As I recorded each new question, I posed it to my parents separately. Then I waited patiently for their responses.

My parents seemed to sincerely enjoy responding to each question, and soon we were strolling down memory lane collecting little jewels about their lives along the way. It was a terrific way to spend the afternoon.

Having a chance to record your own legacy journal is something everyone should have the opportunity to do. This journal can be a conversation starter, one that could serve as a well-documented piece of your own life history. It will have you reminiscing about days gone by, celebrating milestones, and thinking about the future. It is something you and your loved ones can enjoy together now, and later it can become a keepsake of memories to be passed down and treasured by future generations.

Life is a precious gift and one that deserves to be recorded, shared and cherished. We shouldn't wait until someone has passed to celebrate their life when we have a chance to celebrate it today. What better gift to leave behind for those you love than a record of your life from your perspective.

This *Celebration of Life: A Legacy Journal* was created so you too could experience the joys of celebrating a life well lived, a journey as unique and wonderful as the person or persons being celebrated. Colorable images have been sprinkled throughout for added enjoyment as you ponder the many thought provoking questions your new journal contains. May this journaling experience bless you, and those you choose to share it with, as much as it has blessed me.

Sincerely,

Sharon Purtill

Celebration of Life

A Legacy Journal

Table of Contents

This journal documents the life of:

_____

Just for fun: Looking up my name I discovered it to mean:

_____

The date this journal was started: /   /

Chapter One

Where It All Began

Where It All Began

My Place of Birth: _____

My Date of Birth: _____

What do I think of when I think about the place I was born?

_____

_____

_____

_____

_____

_____

A description of my childhood home:

_____

_____

_____

_____

_____

_____

_____

_____

Here are some of my earliest childhood memories:

Who else shares a birthday with me? Googling my birthday turned up these famous names:

_____

_____

_____

_____

_____

_____

_____

_____

When I think of childhood birthdays or holidays, this one stands out in my mind:

_____

_____

_____

_____

_____

_____

_____

_____

_____

_____

_____

_____

_____

_____

_____

_____

When I was a child, what did I dream about being when I grew up?

_____

_____

_____

_____

_____

Did that dream ever change and if so when?

_____

_____

_____

_____

_____

_____

_____

_____

If I could go back, what would I tell myself about the dreams I had as a youngster?

_____

_____

_____

_____

_____

_____

_____

_____

_____

Did I have nicknames when I was younger? If so, what were they? Who gave them to me? Have they stuck?

_____

_____

_____

_____

_____

_____

_____

_____

What was one of the greatest lessons from my childhood?

_____

_____

_____

_____

_____

_____

_____

_____

_____

_____

_____

_____

_____

What was the most challenging time I had as a child?

_____
_____
_____
_____
_____
_____
_____
_____
_____
_____

How did this challenging time affect me as I grew older?

_____
_____
_____
_____
_____
_____
_____
_____
_____
_____
_____

If I had the opportunity to change something about my early years, what would it be?

How would I describe myself as a person today?

Does how I feel others see me differ from how I see myself? If so how?

_____
_____
_____
_____
_____
_____
_____
_____
_____
_____
_____

How different or similar am I today than the person I envisioned I would be at this stage in my life?

_____
_____
_____
_____
_____
_____
_____
_____
_____
_____
_____
_____
_____
_____

Just for fun, here are a few of my favorite things:

Favorite Color:

_____

Favorite Song or Artist:

_____

Favorite Book:

_____

Favorite Movie:

_____

Favorite Restaurant:

_____

A few more of my favorites include:

_____
_____
_____
_____
_____
_____
_____
_____
_____

Chapter Two

Gratitude

Gratitude

The things I love about my life:

A time I am most appreciative for is when:

A time in my life when I didn't feel so grateful was when:

_____

_____

_____

_____

_____

_____

_____

_____

_____

_____

_____

_____

Looking back over that time, are there lessons I can find appreciation for?
If so, what are they?

_____

_____

_____

_____

_____

_____

_____

_____

_____

_____

_____

Who do I feel has been the most influential person in my life thus far and how have they influenced me?

The people I am most grateful for in my life and why:

The places I am most grateful for and why:

_____
_____
_____
_____
_____
_____
_____
_____
_____
_____
_____
_____
_____
_____
_____

Write about a place I went to when I was younger to find solace.

_____
_____
_____
_____
_____
_____
_____
_____
_____
_____

Write a personal note of gratitude to one person I owe a debt of gratitude towards.

Write about a time someone expressed gratitude to me and what they were thanking me for.

_____
_____
_____
_____
_____
_____
_____
_____
_____
_____
_____
_____
_____
_____

How do I believe expressing gratitude impacts our lives?

_____
_____
_____
_____
_____
_____
_____
_____
_____
_____
_____
_____
_____

What natural beauty have I experienced in my life and how did it make me feel?

Write about a time when I felt at peace.

Who do I know that practices gratitude on a regular basis and what have I learned from that person?

What else would I like to say about gratitude?

Chapter Three

Love, Family & Friends

Love, Family & Friends

What love means to me:

_____

_____

_____

_____

_____

_____

_____

_____

What family means to me:

_____

_____

_____

_____

_____

_____

_____

_____

What true friendship means to me:

_____

_____

_____

_____

_____

_____

_____

When I reflect on the greatest love of my life, this is what I think about:

_____
_____
_____
_____
_____
_____
_____
_____
_____
_____
_____
_____
_____
_____
_____
_____

A romantic moment that I will always remember:

_____
_____
_____
_____
_____
_____
_____
_____
_____

Some people come into my life for a season, not a lifetime. Here is a bit about one of those people and what their season of friendship meant to me.

My longest friendship has been with _____

We have been friends since _____

Here is a little about our friendship and what it means to me:

_____

_____

_____

_____

_____

_____

_____

_____

_____

_____

_____

_____

_____

_____

_____

_____

_____

_____

_____

_____

_____

_____

_____

_____

_____

_____

_____

_____

_____

When I think about the relationships of others, whose relationship do I admire most and why?

The person or persons I admire most in the world and why I look up to them:

_____

_____

_____

_____

_____

_____

_____

_____

_____

_____

_____

_____

_____

_____

_____

_____

_____

_____

_____

_____

_____

_____

_____

_____

_____

_____

_____

_____

_____

_____

If I could rewrite history, are there any relationships I would contribute to differently? If so, which one(s) and what would I change?

Is there someone in my family or life that I would describe as being like oil and water to me? Who would that be and what have I learned from our relationship?

Is there a relationship that has come and gone from my life that I miss on a regular basis? Write a little about that:

Write about an animal friend(s), how and when they came into my life and the meaningfulness of the bond we have shared.

The remainder of this chapter
is dedicated to people
I love and care about.

Note: There are four separate pages for each
person's dedication and enough pages
for creating fourteen dedications.

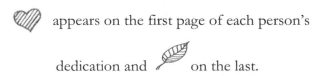

appears on the first page of each person's

dedication and   on the last.

Want to skip the dedication section for now?
If so, the next chapter begins on page 105.

A dedication to: _____

What I love most about you is:

_____
_____
_____
_____
_____
_____
_____

Here are just a few of the ways you have affected my life and the lessons
you have taught me:

_____
_____
_____
_____
_____
_____
_____

When I think of you, I am most proud of:

_____
_____
_____
_____
_____
_____
_____

Something I hope you have learned from me is:

My favorite memory of you is:

Something I want you to know and always remember is:

_____
_____
_____
_____
_____
_____
_____
_____
_____
_____

My greatest hope for your future is:

_____
_____
_____
_____
_____
_____
_____
_____
_____
_____
_____
_____
_____
_____
_____

Use this page to share additional thoughts, memories and/or photos.

51

A dedication to: _____

What I love most about you is:

_____
_____
_____
_____
_____
_____
_____
_____

Here are just a few of the ways you have affected my life and the lessons
you have taught me:

_____
_____
_____
_____
_____
_____
_____

When I think of you, I am most proud of:

_____
_____
_____
_____
_____
_____

Something I hope you have learned from me is:

My favorite memory of you is:

Something I want you to know and always remember is:

_____
_____
_____
_____
_____
_____
_____
_____
_____
_____

My greatest hope for your future is:

_____
_____
_____
_____
_____
_____
_____
_____
_____
_____
_____
_____
_____
_____

Use this page to share additional thoughts, memories and/or photos.

A dedication to: _____

What I love most about you is:

_____
_____
_____
_____
_____
_____
_____
_____

Here are just a few of the ways you have affected my life and the lessons you have taught me:

_____
_____
_____
_____
_____
_____
_____

When I think of you, I am most proud of:

_____
_____
_____
_____
_____
_____

Something I hope you have learned from me is:

My favorite memory of you is:

Something I want you to know and always remember is:

_____
_____
_____
_____
_____
_____
_____
_____
_____

My greatest hope for your future is:

_____
_____
_____
_____
_____
_____
_____
_____
_____
_____
_____
_____
_____
_____

Use this page to share additional thoughts, memories and/or photos.

A dedication to: _____

What I love most about you is:

_____
_____
_____
_____
_____
_____
_____
_____

Here are just a few of the ways you have affected my life and the lessons you have taught me:

_____
_____
_____
_____
_____
_____
_____

When I think of you, I am most proud of:

_____
_____
_____
_____
_____
_____

Something I hope you have learned from me is:

My favorite memory of you is:

Something I want you to know and always remember is:

_____
_____
_____
_____
_____
_____
_____
_____
_____
_____

My greatest hope for your future is:

_____
_____
_____
_____
_____
_____
_____
_____
_____
_____
_____
_____
_____
_____
_____
_____

Use this page to share additional thoughts, memories and/or photos.

A dedication to: _____

What I love most about you is:

_____
_____
_____
_____
_____
_____
_____
_____

Here are just a few of the ways you have affected my life and the lessons you have taught me:

_____
_____
_____
_____
_____
_____
_____
_____

When I think of you, I am most proud of:

_____
_____
_____
_____
_____
_____
_____
_____

Something I hope you have learned from me is:

My favorite memory of you is:

Something I want you to know and always remember is:

_____

_____

_____

_____

_____

_____

_____

_____

_____

_____

My greatest hope for your future is:

_____

_____

_____

_____

_____

_____

_____

_____

_____

_____

_____

_____

_____

_____

_____

Use this page to share additional thoughts, memories and/or photos.

A dedication to: _____

What I love most about you is:

_____
_____
_____
_____
_____
_____
_____
_____

Here are just a few of the ways you have affected my life and the lessons you have taught me:

_____
_____
_____
_____
_____
_____
_____
_____

When I think of you, I am most proud of:

_____
_____
_____
_____
_____
_____

Something I hope you have learned from me is:

My favorite memory of you is:

Something I want you to know and always remember is:

_____
_____
_____
_____
_____
_____
_____
_____
_____

My greatest hope for your future is:

_____
_____
_____
_____
_____
_____
_____
_____
_____
_____
_____
_____
_____
_____
_____

Use this page to share additional thoughts, memories and/or photos.

A dedication to: _____

What I love most about you is:

_____
_____
_____
_____
_____
_____
_____

Here are just a few of the ways you have affected my life and the lessons you have taught me:

_____
_____
_____
_____
_____
_____
_____

When I think of you, I am most proud of:

_____
_____
_____
_____
_____
_____

Something I hope you have learned from me is:

_____
_____
_____
_____
_____
_____

My favorite memory of you is:

_____
_____
_____
_____
_____
_____
_____
_____
_____
_____
_____
_____
_____
_____
_____

Something I want you to know and always remember is:

_____
_____
_____
_____
_____
_____
_____
_____
_____
_____

My greatest hope for your future is:

_____
_____
_____
_____
_____
_____
_____
_____
_____
_____
_____
_____
_____
_____
_____
_____
_____

Use this page to share additional thoughts, memories and/or photos.

A dedication to: _____

What I love most about you is:

_____
_____
_____
_____
_____
_____
_____
_____

Here are just a few of the ways you have affected my life and the lessons you have taught me:

_____
_____
_____
_____
_____
_____
_____
_____

When I think of you, I am most proud of:

_____
_____
_____
_____
_____
_____

Something I hope you have learned from me is:

My favorite memory of you is:

Something I want you to know and always remember is:

_____
_____
_____
_____
_____
_____
_____
_____
_____

My greatest hope for your future is:

_____
_____
_____
_____
_____
_____
_____
_____
_____
_____
_____
_____
_____
_____
_____
_____

Use this page to share additional thoughts, memories and/or photos.

A dedication to: _____

What I love most about you is:

_____
_____
_____
_____
_____
_____
_____
_____

Here are just a few of the ways you have affected my life and the lessons
you have taught me:

_____
_____
_____
_____
_____
_____
_____
_____

When I think of you, I am most proud of:

_____
_____
_____
_____
_____
_____

Something I hope you have learned from me is:

My favorite memory of you is:

Something I want you to know and always remember is:

_____

_____

_____

_____

_____

_____

_____

_____

_____

_____

My greatest hope for your future is:

_____

_____

_____

_____

_____

_____

_____

_____

_____

_____

_____

_____

_____

_____

Use this page to share additional thoughts, memories and/or photos.

A dedication to: _____

What I love most about you is:

_____
_____
_____
_____
_____
_____
_____
_____

Here are just a few of the ways you have affected my life and the lessons you have taught me:

_____
_____
_____
_____
_____
_____
_____

When I think of you, I am most proud of:

_____
_____
_____
_____
_____
_____
_____

Something I hope you have learned from me is:

My favorite memory of you is:

Something I want you to know and always remember is:

_____
_____
_____
_____
_____
_____
_____
_____
_____

My greatest hope for your future is:

_____
_____
_____
_____
_____
_____
_____
_____
_____
_____
_____
_____
_____
_____
_____
_____

Use this page to share additional thoughts, memories and/or photos.

A dedication to: _____

What I love most about you is:

_____
_____
_____
_____
_____
_____
_____
_____

Here are just a few of the ways you have affected my life and the lessons
you have taught me:

_____
_____
_____
_____
_____
_____
_____
_____

When I think of you, I am most proud of:

_____
_____
_____
_____
_____
_____
_____

Something I hope you have learned from me is:

My favorite memory of you is:

Something I want you to know and always remember is:

_____
_____
_____
_____
_____
_____
_____
_____
_____
_____
_____

My greatest hope for your future is:

_____
_____
_____
_____
_____
_____
_____
_____
_____
_____
_____
_____
_____
_____
_____
_____

Use this page to share additional thoughts, memories and/or photos.

A dedication to: _____

What I love most about you is:

_____

_____

_____

_____

_____

_____

_____

Here are just a few of the ways you have affected my life and the lessons you have taught me:

_____

_____

_____

_____

_____

_____

_____

When I think of you, I am most proud of:

_____

_____

_____

_____

_____

_____

Something I hope you have learned from me is:

My favorite memory of you is:

Something I want you to know and always remember is:

_____
_____
_____
_____
_____
_____
_____
_____
_____
_____

My greatest hope for your future is:

_____
_____
_____
_____
_____
_____
_____
_____
_____
_____
_____
_____
_____
_____
_____
_____

Use this page to share additional thoughts, memories and/or photos.

A dedication to: _____

What I love most about you is:

_____
_____
_____
_____
_____
_____
_____

Here are just a few of the ways you have affected my life and the lessons you have taught me:

_____
_____
_____
_____
_____
_____
_____

When I think of you, I am most proud of:

_____
_____
_____
_____
_____
_____

Something I hope you have learned from me is:

_____

_____

_____

_____

_____

_____

_____

My favorite memory of you is:

_____

_____

_____

_____

_____

_____

_____

_____

_____

_____

_____

_____

_____

_____

_____

_____

Something I want you to know and always remember is:

_____
_____
_____
_____
_____
_____
_____
_____
_____
_____

My greatest hope for your future is:

_____
_____
_____
_____
_____
_____
_____
_____
_____
_____
_____
_____
_____
_____
_____
_____
_____

Use this page to share additional thoughts, memories and/or photos.

A dedication to: _____

What I love most about you is:

_____
_____
_____
_____
_____
_____
_____
_____

Here are just a few of the ways you have affected my life and the lessons you have taught me:

_____
_____
_____
_____
_____
_____
_____
_____

When I think of you, I am most proud of:

_____
_____
_____
_____
_____
_____

Something I hope you have learned from me is:

My favorite memory of you is:

Something I want you to know and always remember is:

_____
_____
_____
_____
_____
_____
_____
_____
_____

My greatest hope for your future is:

_____
_____
_____
_____
_____
_____
_____
_____
_____
_____
_____
_____
_____
_____

Use this page to share additional thoughts, memories and/or photos.

Chapter Four

Happiness & Joy

- IT'S A -

New
day

Happiness

Here is how I define happiness:

_____

_____

_____

_____

_____

_____

_____

_____

_____

_____

_____

_____

_____

_____

_____

_____

_____

_____

_____

_____

_____

When am I happiest?

As I reflect back over my life, my happiest memory so far is:

_____

_____

_____

_____

_____

_____

_____

_____

_____

_____

_____

_____

_____

_____

_____

_____

_____

_____

_____

_____

_____

_____

_____

_____

_____

_____

_____

What are some of the simple things in life that bring me happiness?

What is the key to happiness?

What, if anything, is blocking my ability to find more happiness in my life and how can I work to change that?

Here is how I define joy:

_____

_____

_____

_____

_____

_____

_____

_____

_____

Describe a time I shed tears of joy. What was happening and why do I think it impacted me the way it did?

When or where do I experience my greatest joy? Is it when I am alone in nature? Listening to music? Singing in the shower?
Here are my experiences:

Are there certain people in my life who elevate my joy? If so, who are they, and how do they bring joy into my life?

In contrast, was there a time in my life when I struggled to find joy? What was going on with me then, and what, if anything, did that experience teach me about myself?

My funniest memory is:

_____

_____

_____

_____

_____

_____

_____

_____

_____

I recall a time I did something crazy or silly that had others laughing. Here is what happened:

_____

_____

_____

_____

_____

_____

_____

_____

_____

_____

_____

_____

_____

_____

Who is the most joyous person I know and what do I love about them?

_____

_____

_____

_____

_____

_____

_____

Ways I believe I have brought joy and happiness to others:

_____

_____

_____

_____

_____

_____

_____

_____

_____

_____

_____

_____

_____

_____

_____

_____

Laughter is like medicine to the soul. Write about a time this rang true for me:

_____
_____
_____
_____
_____
_____
_____
_____
_____
_____
_____
_____
_____
_____
_____

My most embarrassing moment:

_____
_____
_____
_____
_____
_____
_____
_____
_____
_____
_____

I have moved _____ times in my life. I enjoyed living in
_____ the most and here is why:

_____

_____

_____

_____

_____

_____

_____

_____

_____

_____

_____

_____

_____

How I believe we can achieve more joy in the world:

_____

_____

_____

_____

_____

_____

_____

_____

_____

_____

_____

Chapter Five

Dreams & Goals

the best
Dreams
-HAPPEN-
when you are
awake

How important are dreams and goals to me and why?

_____
_____
_____
_____
_____
_____
_____
_____
_____
_____

What does my dream home look like?

_____
_____
_____
_____
_____
_____
_____
_____
_____
_____
_____
_____

Describe a specific dream I have fulfilled in my life and how the fulfillment of that dream has affected me.

Describe a specific dream I have had for my life that has not yet been fulfilled and what this dream means to me.

_____

_____

_____

_____

_____

_____

_____

_____

_____

_____

_____

_____

_____

_____

_____

_____

_____

_____

_____

_____

_____

_____

_____

_____

_____

What place(s) would I like to visit, and why? What do I think I would enjoy about visiting there?

_____

_____

_____

_____

_____

_____

_____

_____

_____

_____

_____

_____

_____

What have my dreams taught me about myself?

Here are my thoughts on goals and how much or how little they have influenced my life thus far:

_____

_____

_____

_____

_____

_____

_____

_____

_____

_____

_____

_____

_____

_____

_____

_____

_____

_____

_____

_____

_____

_____

What was the last goal I set for myself? Did I achieve it? Describe this experience below.

What goal have I achieved, that above all others gave me the most satisfaction? What did I learn from this experience?

Three things I need to take action on right now:

1. _____

2. _____

3. _____

Was there something I strived for, that once I achieved it, I felt it wasn't worth the time and effort? What was it and what did this experience teach me?

What is holding me back from fulfilling my remaining dreams and goals?

How can I push past these roadblocks and attain my dreams?

List 5 things I will strive to accomplish in the next _____ months.

1. _____

2. _____

3. _____

4. _____

5. _____

A list of ten things I have already accomplished in my lifetime:

1. _____

2. _____

3. _____

4. _____

5. _____

6. _____

7. _____

8. _____

9. _____

10. _____

Wow! That's pretty awesome.

Chapter Six

Life Lessons

Life can take us down unexpected paths.
It can surprise us, challenge us,
enlighten us, and provide us with
opportunities we didn't expect or plan for.

Life's unexpected events, whether
negative or positive, can enrich
our experience and shape us
into the people we become.

One of the most valuable life lessons I've learned is:

What has been my proudest moment so far?

_____

_____

_____

_____

_____

_____

_____

The older I get, the wiser I become. If I could go back in time and give some advice to my younger self, what advice would I offer?

_____

_____

_____

_____

_____

_____

_____

_____

_____

_____

_____

_____

_____

_____

_____

_____

Navigating life is easier when we understand our weaknesses. Here are a few of mine:

_____
_____
_____
_____
_____
_____
_____
_____
_____
_____

What have my weaknesses taught me about life?

_____
_____
_____
_____
_____
_____
_____
_____
_____
_____
_____
_____
_____

Write about a time I experienced rejection. How did I react and what did I learn from my experience?

What is my greatest fear or phobia?

_____

_____

_____

_____

_____

_____

Write about a time I experienced fear. What happened? How did I overcome it? And what did I learn from my experience?

_____

_____

_____

_____

_____

_____

_____

_____

_____

_____

_____

_____

_____

_____

_____

Was there a time in my life where I fought hard for something I believed in? If so, what was that experience like for me?

Looking back, what things in my past do I wish I put less focus on?

_____
_____
_____
_____
_____
_____
_____
_____
_____
_____

What things in my past do I wish I had focused on more?

_____
_____
_____
_____
_____
_____
_____
_____
_____
_____
_____

Luck – some believe in luck and others do not. Here is what I have to say
about luck:

Write about a time I witnessed a random act of kindness or love and what that experience was like:

_____
_____
_____
_____
_____
_____
_____
_____
_____
_____

Write about a time I witnessed discrimination or hate and what that experience was like:

_____
_____
_____
_____
_____
_____
_____
_____
_____
_____

What lessons have I learned from witnessing the extremes in our world?

_____
_____
_____
_____
_____
_____
_____
_____
_____
_____
_____
_____
_____
_____
_____

If it was my job to teach others about life, what would I say are the five most important things to remember?

1. _____

2. _____

3. _____

4. _____

5. _____

Sometimes we lose focus of what is really important. What can I do to ensure that doesn't happen from this point forward?

Other thoughts I'd like to share about the life lessons I've learned:

Chapter Seven

Legacy

A legacy is something we will all leave behind.
The type of legacy we leave is up to each of
us and there is no better time to think about
our legacy than while we are still living.

Here is what I believe my life's purpose is:

Here is what I hope my legacy will look like?

What is something I know about my family's history that others may be unaware of?

Milestones I've reached in my life that have had great meaning for me:

_____
_____
_____
_____
_____
_____
_____
_____
_____
_____
_____

Here is what I would like to focus on doing or being for the remainder of my life:

_____
_____
_____
_____
_____
_____
_____
_____
_____
_____
_____
_____
_____
_____

What was my favourite age to be and what did I like about being that age?

Here are five things most people don't know about me:

1. _____

_____

_____

_____

2. _____

_____

_____

_____

3. _____

_____

_____

_____

4. _____

_____

_____

_____

5. _____

_____

_____

_____

Here are my thoughts on what happens after we leave this life:

_____

_____

_____

_____

_____

_____

_____

Whether it is tomorrow, or many years in the future, when my time comes to leave this earth, I'd like others to know that I have thought about being an organ donor. Here is what I'd like my loved ones to know about that:

_____

_____

_____

_____

_____

_____

I have thought about the vessel that has served as my body for the time I have been on this earth. Some people wish to be cremated and some people wish to be buried. Here are my personal thoughts on what I would like to happen to my own body after I pass.

_____

_____

_____

_____

_____

If I have written or recorded a final will and testament I have recorded below the instructions on where that can be found. I have also noted any additional information pertaining to this here.

Other thoughts and things I would like to share about my legacy:

_____

_____

_____

_____

_____

_____

_____

_____

_____

_____

_____

_____

_____

_____

_____

_____

_____

_____

_____

_____

_____

_____

_____

_____

_____

_____

_____

_____

_____

_____

Other Notes & Random Stuff

Finished This Journal On

/ /

Made in United States
Orlando, FL
09 April 2024

45617971R00096